*Poems*

# WHISPERS IN THE WIND: ETERNITY & SOUL

*J. Chester*

*For information, address J's Personal Services LLC via email.*
*Jarvaris Chester*
*jspersonalservicesllc@gmail.com*
*Library of Congress Cataloging -in- Publication Data has been applied for.*
*Hard Cover ISBN: 979-8-9884648-6-0*
*Paperback ISBN: 979-8-9884648-8-4*
*#002 Edition 2026*

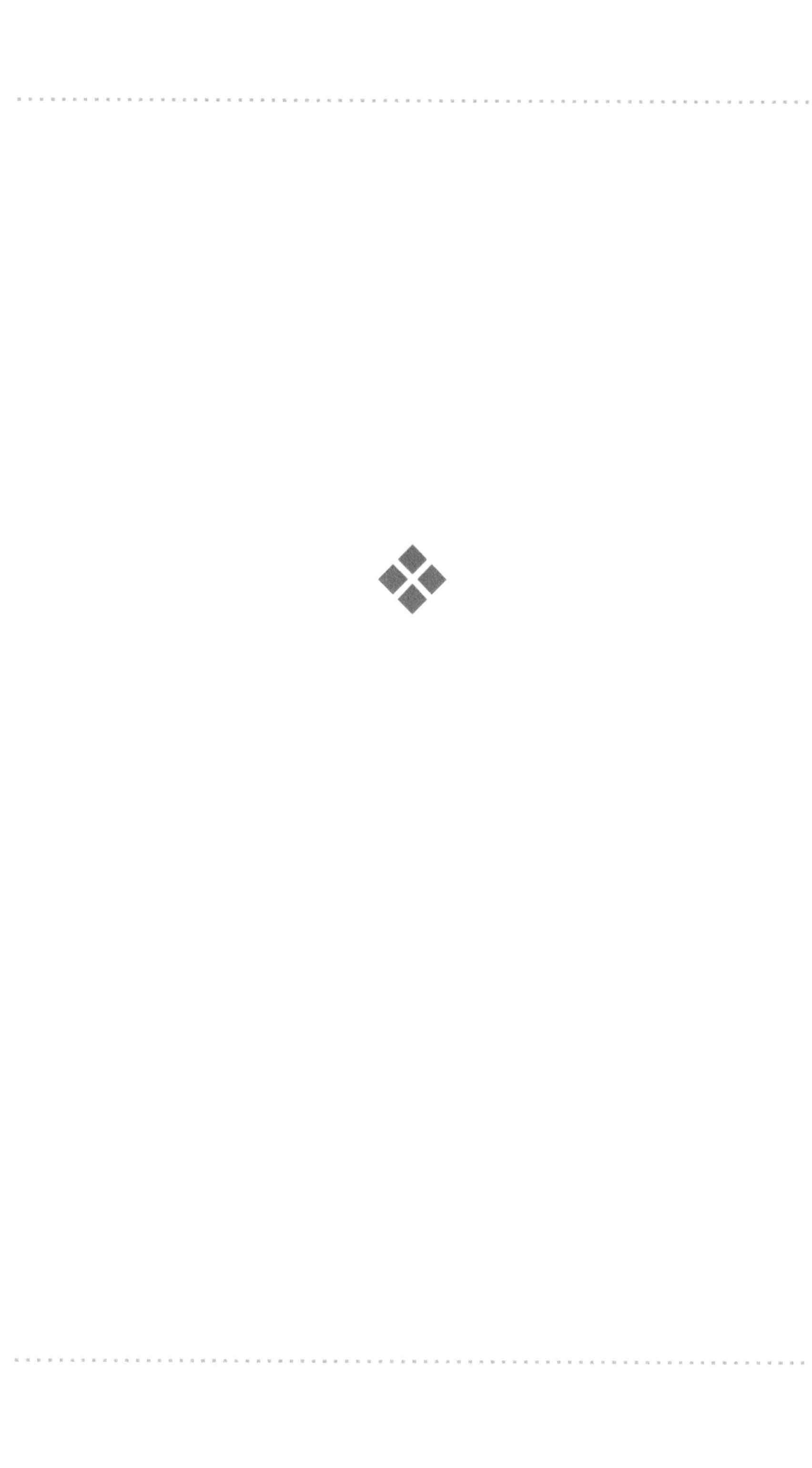

*And we Begin*

## *Preface*

*These poems came from living ~*

*from loving badly and ... well,*

*from the kind of hurt that teaches you something..*

*and the kind that just hurts.*

*They are not tidy.*

*Neither is a life.*

*Read them slowly. Find the one that knows your name.*

*Fear will come anyway ~*

*let it sit in the passenger seat ...*

*It does not get to drive.*

*She watched couples through coffee shop windows*

*like someone watching a film ..*

*In a language she almost understood.*

*She knew the word.*

*She'd said it, even ~*

*but it never quite landed*

*anywhere soft.*

*Just breathe.*

*1, 2, 3 ~ in, hold, let go.*

*That's all. Just that.*

*Before the to-do list,*

*before the worry about the thing*

*you can't control ~*

*One breath in.*

*One breath out.*

*You are still here.*

*That's not nothing.*

*That's everything.*

*It doesn't look like transformation*

*from the inside.*

*From the inside it looks like*

*being very still in the dark*

*and not knowing why.*

*But something is happening.*

*Something always is.*

*Good things come later.*

*Trust the cocoon.*

*Every scar ~*

*is a door you walked through*

*when you thought you couldn't.*

*Look at how many doors*

*are behind you now.*

*You've been this tired before.*

*You kept going before.*

*Look in the mirror.*

*That's not someone who gives up.*

*That's someone who keeps going.*

*They never touch*

*but they never lose each other either ~*

*the sun always leaving the sky*

*exactly warm enough for the moon to arrive.*

*This is what balance looks like:*

*not both things at once,*

*but each thing in its season,*

*trusting the other is coming.*

*The canvas is not ruined.*

*It's just not finished.*

*You don't have to fight the feeling.*

*You don't have to fix it.*

*Just sit with it like a storm outside ~*

*watch it through the screen door.*

*Notice how it moves.*

*Notice how it passes.*

*Fear is weather.*

*You are the house.*

*Morning, and the sheets are undisturbed.*

*No residue of someone who made me small.*

*I didn't know how heavy*

*I'd been carrying that*

*until I set it down.*

*The sun comes in differently now ~*

*like it's allowed.*

*I am allowed.*

*Love should not leave bruises*

*you can't see.*

*If it costs you your voice,*

*your sleep, your sense of what is real ~*

*that's not love.*

*That's a lease you've been paying*

*on a place that was never home.*

*You are allowed to leave.*

*You are allowed to want better.*

*You deserve a love*

*that makes you larger, not smaller.*

*Such a small creature*

*to carry that much joy.*

*She doesn't know*

*she's teaching anyone anything ~*

*she just sings because the morning is there*

*and she is in it.*

*What would it be*

*to live like that?*

*To just ~*

*sing, because you're here?*

*It isn't loud.*

*It doesn't announce itself.*

*It's the morning coffee.*

*The laugh that surprises you.*

*The moment of sunlight*

*through a window at the right angle.*

*Joy is not a destination.*

*It's the thing*

*that's been living in the small things*

*all along,*

*waiting for you*

*to notice.*

*Not silver. Not gold.*

*Not the approval of rooms full of people*

*who'll forget my name by Friday.*

*Just this ~*

*the one constant*

*when everything else*

*shifts under my feet.*

*I have stood in storms*

*I should not have survived.*

*Something held me.*

*I know what it was.*

*There's a specific silence*

*that only snow makes ~*

*not empty,*

*full.*

*Like the world pressing pause.*

*Like being given permission*

*to just watch something beautiful happen*

*and not rush it.*

*Children already know this.*

*That's why they run outside.*

*I know it doesn't look like it.*

*I know the path has been strange,*

*and long, and sometimes it felt like a mistake.*

*But look at what you've learned.*

*Look at who you've become*

*in all the places*

*you thought were setbacks.*

*Right here. Right now.*

*This is exactly where you're supposed to be.*

*Let it go.*

*Not because it doesn't matter,*

*but because you matter more*

*than what you're holding.*

*Make room.*

*Make space.*

*Make room for what's coming*

*that hasn't arrived yet*

*because your hands are too full.*

*They come in the night*

*but they're asking about the day ~*

*about what you'd do*

*if you stopped being afraid*

*of wanting things.*

*Pay attention.*

*It's not a distraction.*

*It's instruction.*

*I am here*

*and that is not a small thing.*

*I have a voice.*

*I have a story that belongs*

*to no one else.*

*I am not waiting*

*for someone to confirm this.*

*Full stop.*

*I have felt this presence ~*

*not something I can point to,*

*but something that steadied me*

*when I should have fallen.*

*A warmth in the cold parts.*

*A sense of not being alone*

*in rooms where I was alone.*

*I don't need to explain it.*

*I just need to be grateful.*

*So I am.*

*You hurt me.*

*I'm not going to dress that up.*

*But I'm not going to carry it forever*

*like a stone I found on your property.*

*It's not mine to carry.*

*I forgive you.*

*Not for you ~*

*for the lightness of it.*

*For the way my shoulders feel*

*when I finally put it down.*

*Some days the smile is real*

*and some days it's armor*

*and some days you can't tell the difference ~*

*and that's okay.*

*The smile that hides the pain*

*is still a kind of courage.*

*You are still standing.*

*That matters.*

*Solitude is not the same as lonely.*

*Lonely is wanting someone there.*

*Solitude is choosing the quiet*

*because you've realized*

*you are someone worth spending time with.*

*Come back to yourself here.*

*This is not emptiness.*

*This is refilling.*

*You can't save time.*

*You can't borrow it.*

*You can't get yesterday back*

*no matter how much*

*you're willing to pay for it.*

*But right now ~*

*this moment, this one ~*

*is yours, entirely.*

*What do you want to do with it?*

*Fire gives everything.*

*Ice keeps everything.*

*You need both ~*

*the burning to feel alive,*

*the stillness to preserve*

*what matters.*

*The secret is knowing,*

*which one this moment is asking for.*

*This is not the season for everything.*

*Some seasons are for growing.*

*Some are for resting.*

*Some are for grieving things*

*that needed to be grieved.*

*You are not behind.*

*You are exactly*

*in the season you're in.*

*Let it be what it is.*

*The darkness will tell you*

*it's telling the truth.*

*It isn't.*

*It borrows your voice*

*and uses it against you.*

*It knows exactly what to say…*

*Don't listen.*

*The light is not gone.*

*It's right here.*

*I promise you ~*

*it's right here.*

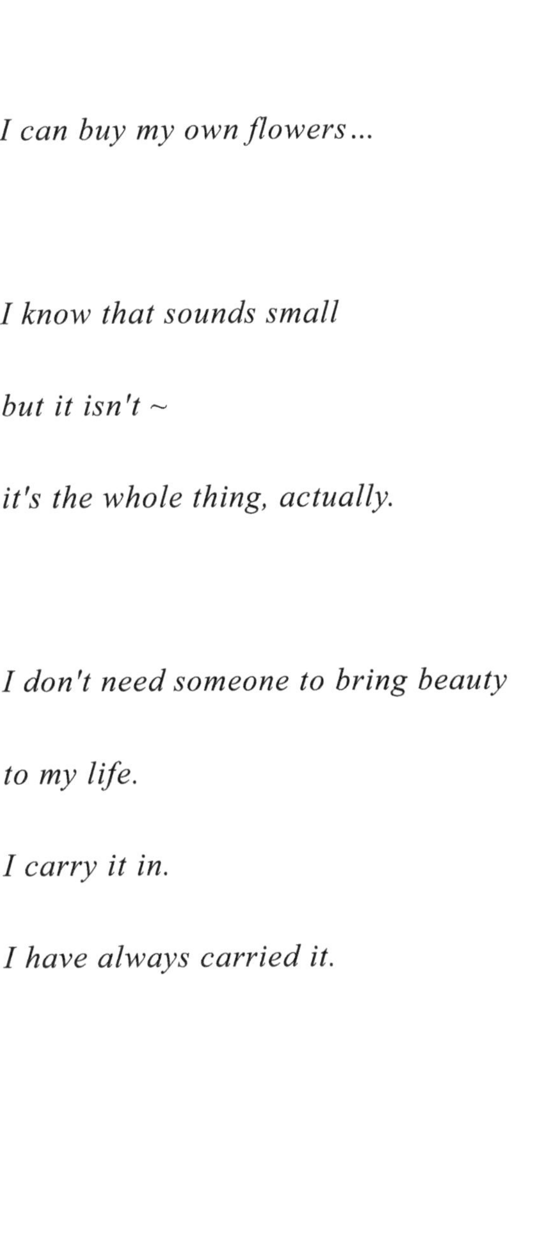

*I can buy my own flowers…*

*I know that sounds small*

*but it isn't ~*

*it's the whole thing, actually.*

*I don't need someone to bring beauty*

*to my life.*

*I carry it in.*

*I have always carried it.*

*I let you go.*

*Not because I stopped caring ~*

*caring was never the problem.*

*The problem was*

*that caring wasn't enough*

*to make it right.*

*I let you go*

*and I let myself*

*start over.*

*That took everything I had.*

*And I'd do it again.*

*You asked for my time*

*like it cost you nothing.*

*It cost me everything.*

*I'm not angry anymore.*

*I'm just careful now.*

*about who I give it to ~*

*This is a space built for light.*

*You can't bring what you're bringing*

*and stay here.*

*Not cruelty.*

*Not that old story you keep telling.*

*Not the weight you want someone else to carry.*

*Leave it at the door*

*or leave.*

*The door is right there.*

*I used to wait for someone*

*to tell me I was enough.*

*Now I know:*

*nobody can hand you that.*

*You have to grow it yourself,*

*in the quiet,*

*the way anything real grows ~*

*slowly, without applause,*

*reaching toward your own light.*

*The crow doesn't apologize*

*for being black,*

*for being loud,*

*for knowing things.*

*She lands where she pleases*

*and looks right at you ~*

*no flinching.*

*I've been practicing that.*

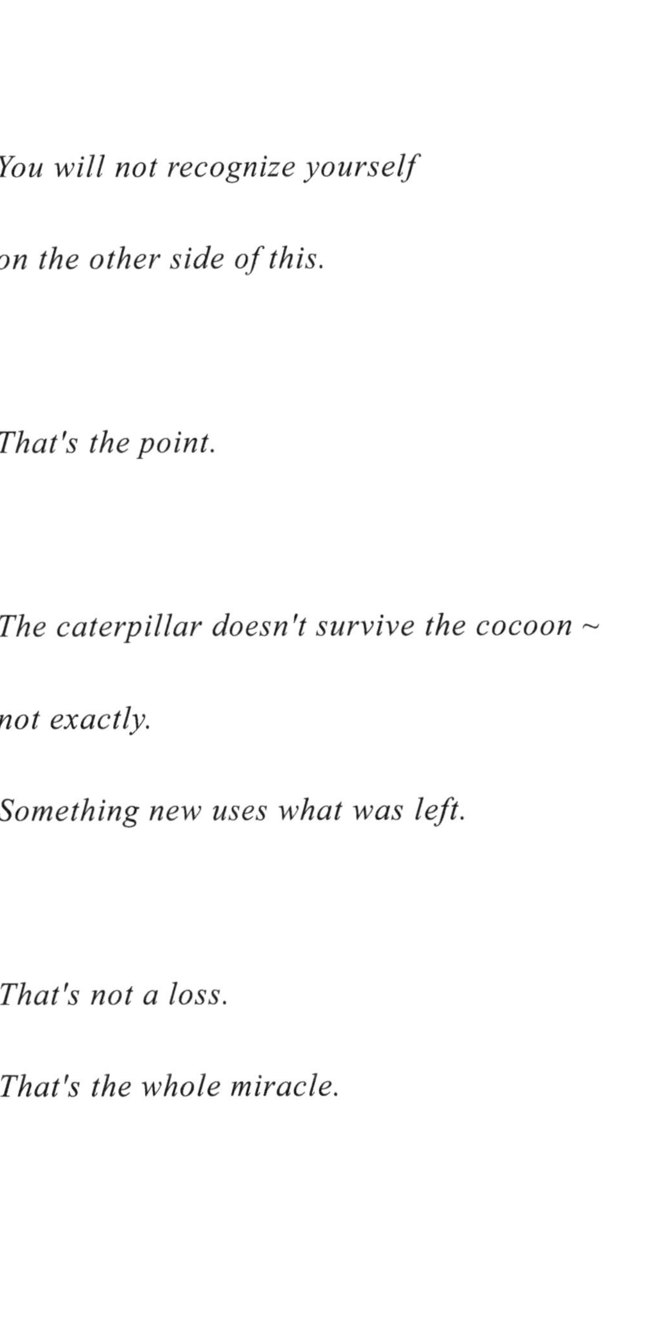

*You will not recognize yourself*

*on the other side of this.*

*That's the point.*

*The caterpillar doesn't survive the cocoon ~*

*not exactly.*

*Something new uses what was left.*

*That's not a loss.*

*That's the whole miracle.*

*The mountain doesn't need the moon*

*and the moon doesn't need the mountain.*

*But each is more beautiful*

*for the other's presence.*

*That's the best kind of relationship ~*

*two whole things*

*that choose each other.*

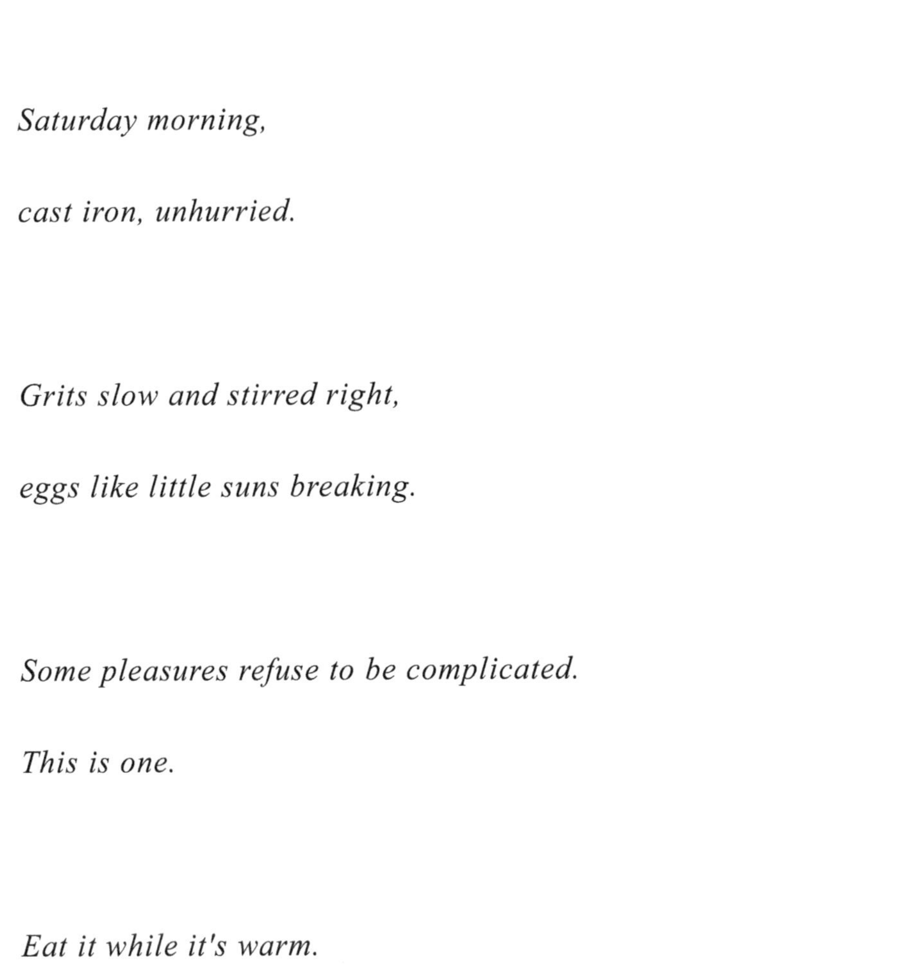

*Saturday morning,*

*cast iron, unhurried.*

*Grits slow and stirred right,*

*eggs like little suns breaking.*

*Some pleasures refuse to be complicated.*

*This is one.*

*Eat it while it's warm.*

*Eat it slow.*

*Yesterday is a place you've already been.*

*Tomorrow is a place that isn't built yet.*

*But today ~*

*today is happening right now,*

*while you're standing in it.*

*What if you lived like that mattered ?*

*They made me question what I saw*

*with my own eyes.*

*That's a particular kind of violence ~*

*not the bruising kind,*

*the erasing kind.*

*But I found my way back*

*to my own knowing.*

*It was still there,*

*patient,*

*waiting for me.*

*I trust myself now.*

*That's what I got out of it.*

*I have been to places in myself*

*I didn't know existed.*

*Dark places.*

*Quiet places.*

*Places I didn't think I'd get back from.*

*And here I am.*

*I am not just someone who endured.*

*I am someone who came back*

*changed,*

*and chose to keep going anyway.*

*That is not small.*

*The cruelest part wasn't the lies.*

*It was how long I worked*

*to make the lies make sense.*

*The day I stopped ~*

*the day I said,* this is not me,

this is what was done to me ~

*that was the day*

*I started coming home*

*to myself.*

*Halfway is not nothing.*

*Halfway is something*

*most people never reach.*

*Rest here a moment.*

*Look at where you started.*

*Feel the distance.*

*Then go.*

*Let them.*

*I've learned that the loudest critics*

*are often the most afraid ~*

*afraid someone else*

*will do the thing*

*they were too scared to try.*

*Their noise is not about me.*

*My work is not about them.*

*I keep going.*

*They catch you off guard ~*

*a song, a smell,*

*the wrong light at the right angle.*

*And for a second*

*you're back there.*

*That's okay.*

*Feel it. Let it move through.*

*It's not the same as being there.*

*You're here now.*

*You made it here.*

*Biological is just a fact of science.*

*Father is something earned.*

*You gave me the first*

*and disappeared.*

*What I needed was the second.*

*I found it ~ in other men,*

*in my own becoming,*

*in the way I learned to father myself*

*when no one else would.*

*I don't need you to understand that.*

*I just need it to be true.*

And it is.

*You gave me to the hard world*
*and thought that was the end of it.*

*It wasn't.*

*I learned the language of hard things.*
*I found my people out there ~*
*the ones who'd also been abandoned,*
*who built something anyway.*

*You thought the wolves would finish me.*
*You didn't know*

*I'd learn to run with them.*

*I used to scan every room.*

*Now I walk in and just ~*

*arrive.*

*I'm not looking for you anymore.*

*I'm not looking for anyone to complete me.*

*I'm complete.*

*That's new.*

*That's mine.*

*You didn't have to stay.*

*That's the part that still gets me ~*

*you didn't have to,*

*and you did.*

*You showed up to the games.*

*You showed up to the arguments.*

*You showed up.*

*That's not biology. That's a choice.*

*You chose me.*

*I don't have the words*

*for what that means.*

*Only this:*

*thank you.*

*Daddy. ~*

*Go outside.*

*No phone. No plan.*

*Let your feet decide.*

*The trees are not in a hurry.*

*The birds don't have a meeting at two.*

*The creek doesn't care*

*what you didn't finish today.*

*You are a body.*

*Let it move.*

*Let the outside air*

*talk sense into you.*

*It usually works.*

*Some days breathing*

*is the whole job.*

*And that's enough.*

*You don't have to have it figured out.*

*You don't have to be okay.*

*You just have to get to the next breath.*

*Then the one after.*

I'll be here.

*I am more than you've seen.*

*I have a whole interior ~*

*rooms you haven't visited,*

*seasons you didn't see,*

*battles that left no mark you could find.*

*I am not defined by your knowing.*

*I am defined by my own.*

*Sometimes I don't speak*

*and it looks like agreement.*

*It's not.*

*Sometimes silence is how I protect*

*what's too important*

*for a room that can't hold it.*

*I know the difference*

*between silence that shrinks me*

*and silence that keeps me whole.*

*I choose accordingly.*

*Everyone else is taken.*

*You, with all your strange,*

*your specific,*

*your one-of-a-kind way*

*of being in the world ~*

*that's not a flaw.*

*That's the whole point.*

*Stop apologizing for your shape.*

*You were made this way on purpose.*

*The thing you're worried about ~*

*most of it won't happen.*

*And if it does,*

*you will handle it*

*the way you've handled every hard thing:*

*imperfectly,*

*eventually,*

*and better than you thought you could.*

*You've survived 100% of your worst days so far.*

*Put the worry down for tonight.*

*Pick it up again tomorrow*

*if you still need it.*

*You probably won't.*

*She sits in the dark*

*not because she's afraid of the light,*

*but because she doesn't need it.*

*She can see perfectly well*

*by what most call nothing.*

*I've been learning from her. The owl ..*

*The cage was built from the inside.*

*I know that now.*

*It took a long time to know that.*

*The lock was never on the outside.*

*The key was in my hand*

*the whole time.*

*I opened it.*

*I'm out.*

*I'm not going back.*

*I will be honest with you.*

*I will show up.*

*I will tell you the truth*

*even when it costs me something.*

*I will not promise you perfect.*

*But I promise you real.*

*That's everything I have.*

*It's yours.*

*Don't go quiet.*

*Whatever they told you ~*

*that you were too much,*

*too loud, too intense,*

*too certain of things they weren't ready to hear ~*

*they were wrong.*

*Your voice belongs in the world.*

*Use it.*

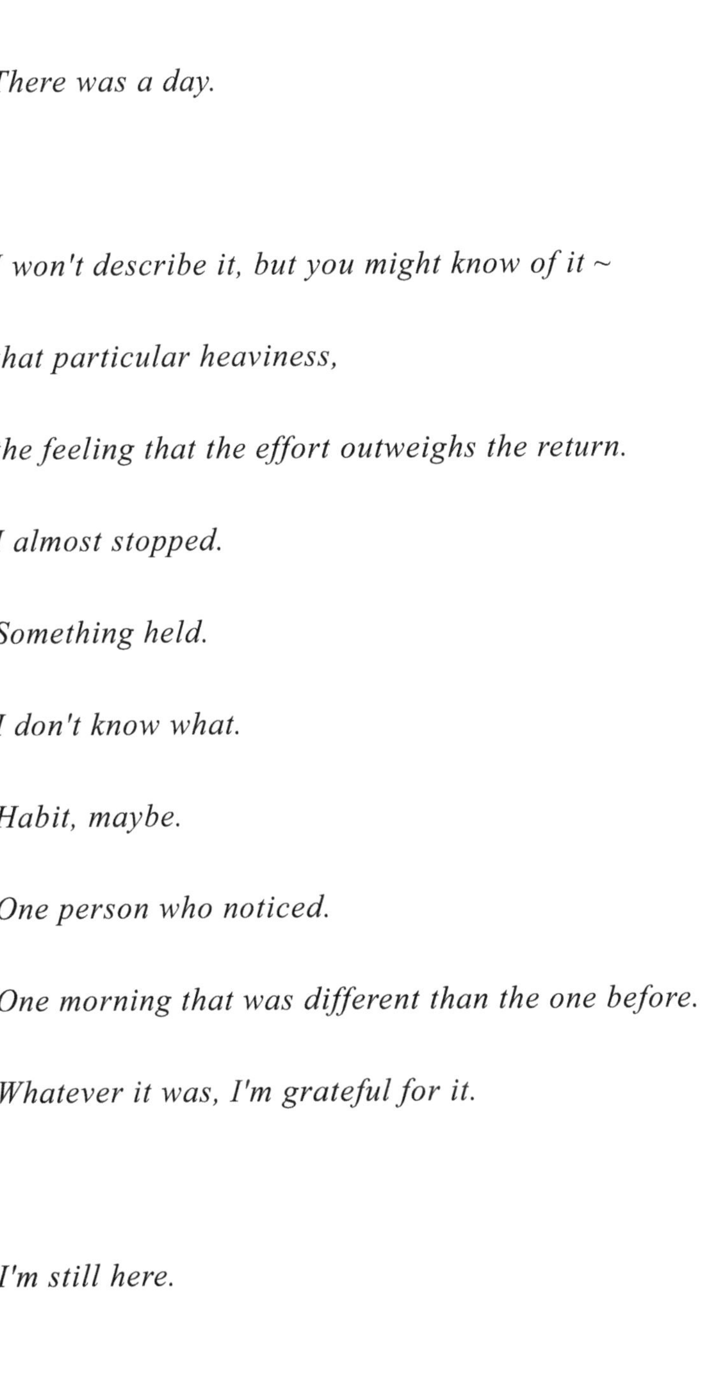

*There was a day.*

*I won't describe it, but you might know of it ~*

*that particular heaviness,*

*the feeling that the effort outweighs the return.*

*I almost stopped.*

*Something held.*

*I don't know what.*

*Habit, maybe.*

*One person who noticed.*

*One morning that was different than the one before.*

*Whatever it was, I'm grateful for it.*

*I'm still here.*

*You are not too much.*

*Whoever told you that was wrong,*

*was small,*

*was threatened by the amount of life*

*you carry.*

*Stand in the center of the room.*

*Speak from your full chest.*

*Take up exactly the amount of space*

*a person takes up.*

*You are a person.*

*This is your space.*

*You are tired, I know.*

*But look at everything you've carried*

*and still ~ still ~*

*showed up.*

*That's not weakness.*

*That's extraordinary.*

*Rest when you need to.*

*You've earned it.*

*And when you're ready,*

*you'll know what's next.*

*You always do.*

*When did you last do something*

*just because it made you glad?*

*Not productive.*

*Not impressive.*

*Not for anyone else.*

*Just ~ glad.*

*Go do that thing.*

*Not everything.*

*Not yet.*

*But more things than it feels like*

*right now, in this moment,*

*when everything is compressed*

*and the walls feel close.*

*Take a breath.*

*Not everything is on fire.*

*Some of it is just hard.*

*Hard is not the end.*

*It's alright.*

*I didn't know I'd feel like this.*

*After the worst of it ~*

*not fine, exactly,*

*but spacious.*

*Like something that was taking up all the room*

*finally left,*

*and light came in where it was.*

*I would not have wished for the pain.*

*But I'm grateful*

*for who it made me.*

*Look how far you've come*

*to stand here*

*and consider stopping.*

*All that distance.*

*All those mornings.*

*Don't let that be for nothing.*

*One more step.*

*Just one.*

*Then the next one.*

*You know how to do this.*

*Not perfect.*

*Not fixed.*

*Not the same as I was before.*

*But here,*

*and breathing,*

*and moving toward something.*

*That's okay.*

*I'm okay.*

*I'm going to be okay.*

*Wherever I bottomed out,*

*you were already there.*

*Every dark room,*

*every time I thought ..*

*there you were.*

*That kind of love*

*doesn't have a name for it.*

*I just hold it.*

*I thought I'd lose color when I got sober.*

*I didn't.*

*The color came back.*

*It had been muted, all that time ~*

*the drinking was supposed to help me feel more*

*but it was just turning the volume down*

*on everything, including me.*

*Now I feel the whole thing.*

*All of it.*

*It's hard sometimes.*

*It's also the most alive I've ever been.*

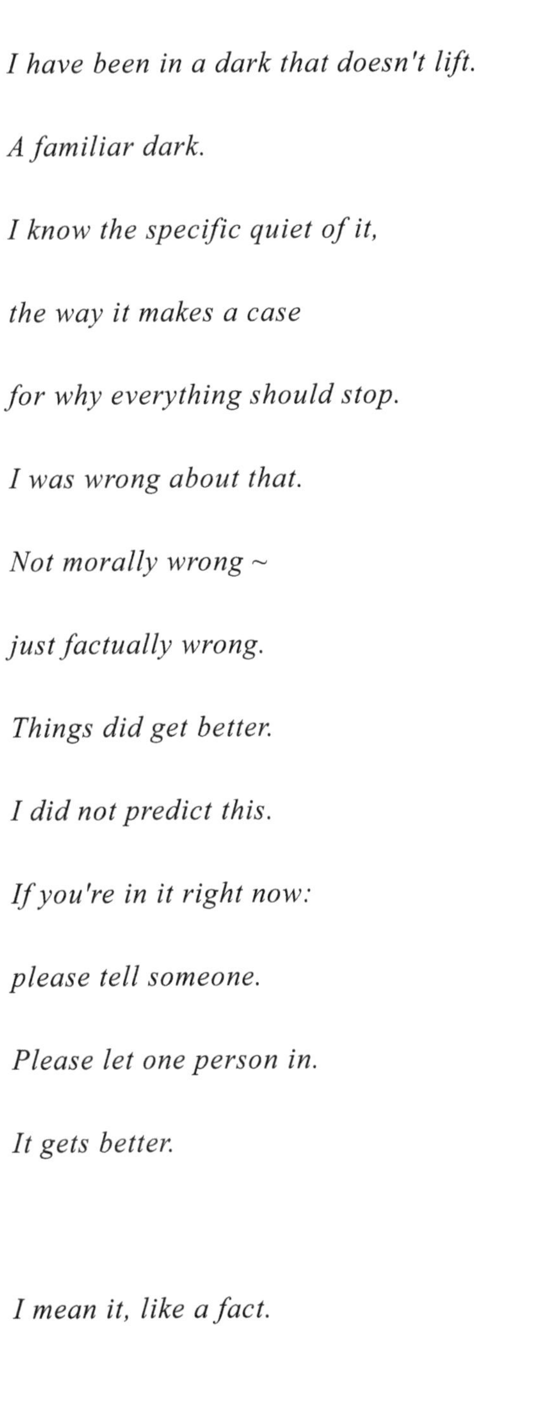

*I have been in a dark that doesn't lift.*

*A familiar dark.*

*I know the specific quiet of it,*

*the way it makes a case*

*for why everything should stop.*

*I was wrong about that.*

*Not morally wrong ~*

*just factually wrong.*

*Things did get better.*

*I did not predict this.*

*If you're in it right now:*

*please tell someone.*

*Please let one person in.*

*It gets better.*

*I mean it, like a fact.*

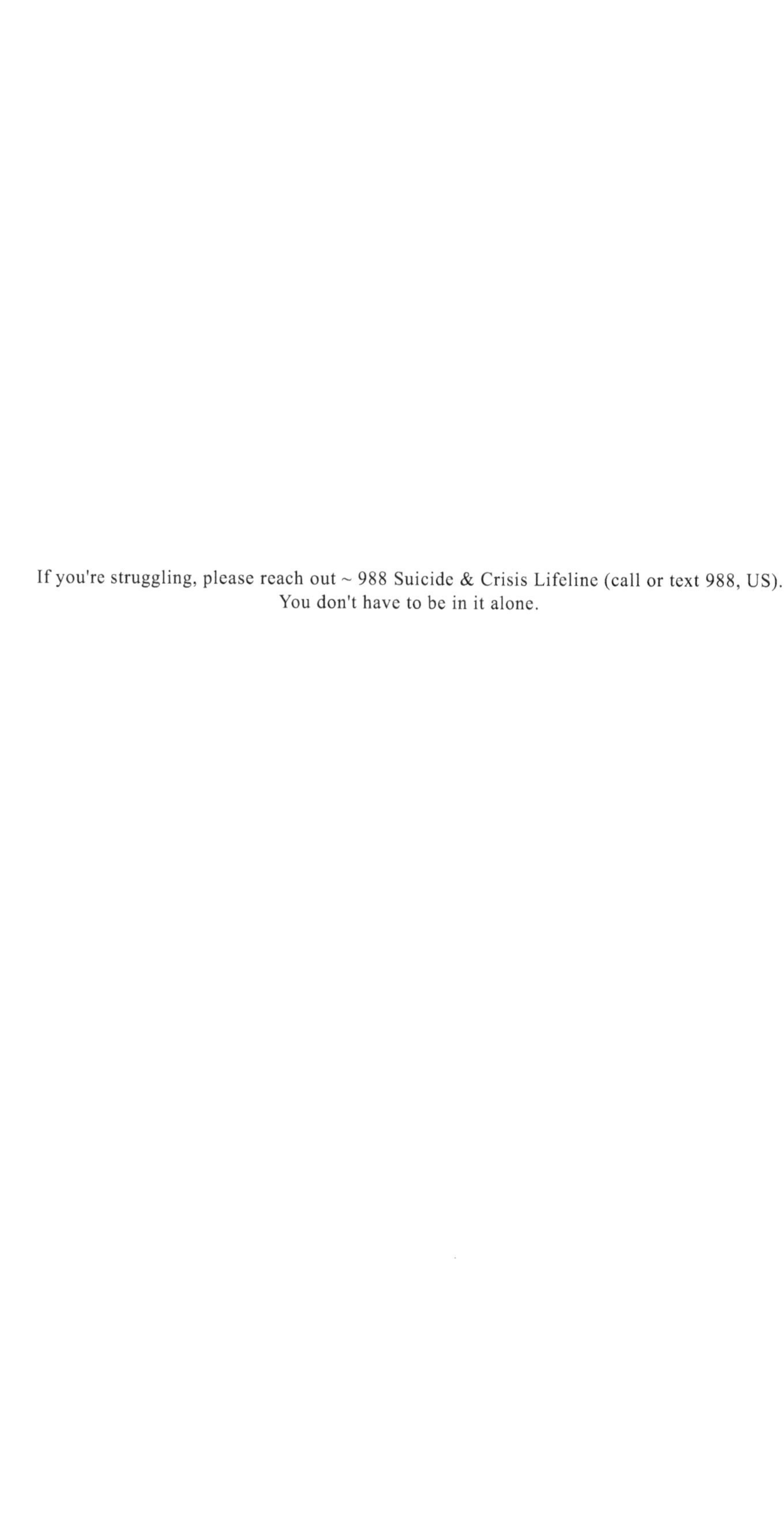

If you're struggling, please reach out ~ 988 Suicide & Crisis Lifeline (call or text 988, US).
You don't have to be in it alone.

*I come from hard things.*

*People who survived*

*what should have broken them.*

*Land that didn't give much*

*but gave what it had.*

*Lessons that came wrapped in pain*

*and taught themselves slowly.*

*I come from all of that.*

*It's in me ~*

*the endurance,*

*the stubbornness,*

*the belief that morning*

*always comes after.*

*I know where I came from.*

*I know what I'm made of.*

*I spent years adding to myself ~*
*more credentials, more effort,*
*more shrinking, more apology ~*
*trying to reach enough.*

*The finish line kept moving.*

*Then one day I just*
*stopped running,*
*and looked at what I already was,*
*and thought: yes.*
*This.*
*This is enough.*
*I am enough.*

*You have been carrying this thought*

*for three days.*

*It is not paying rent.*

*Evict it.*

*Breathe.*

*Step outside if you can.*

*Touch something real ~ bark, water, earth.*

*You are a body with a mind,*

*not a mind with no body.*

*Come back down.*

*You can think again later.*

*Right now, just be.*

*The house is quiet.*

*The coffee is hot.*

*The window is open just enough*

*to let the morning in ~*

*cool and unhurried,*

*carrying the smell of somewhere green.*

*Nothing is required of you yet.*

*Just this.*

*Just here.*

*Just now.*

*The keys are worn*

*in the places my grandmother played.*

*I put my hands there.*

*Play the same songs, almost.*

*The instrument holds everything*

*it has ever been given.*

*So do I.*

*I can still hear it ~*

*that particular spring-and-slap,*

*the sound of summer,*

*of being let in and let out*

*a hundred times a day.*

*Nothing kept us out for long.*

*The door always bounced back.*

*I think about that sometimes.*

*The house that always lets you back in.*

*The door that doesn't hold a grudge.*

*I want to be like that for the people I love.*

*It doesn't rush.*

*Every spring it simply begins ~*

*no announcement,*

*just blossoms appearing*

*like they were always going to.*

*And then the fruit,*

*in its own time,*

*heavy, sweet .. and certain.*

*I am trying to live like that.*

*Unhurried. Certain.*

*Trusting that the fruit*

*will come.*

*This is what it's for ~*

*the fire, the dark ..*

*warm and orange,*

*everyone's eyes a little more open*

*We stayed too late.*

*We always do.*

*These are the nights I remember.*

*The door you came through*

*is not the door you're meant for now.*

*What's behind it*

*looks familiar, yes.*

*That's the trap ~*

*familiar is not the same as good.*

*You know what's back there.*

*You've already lived it.*

*Walk forward.*

*Even slowly.*

*Forward.*

*I'm not going to tell you*

*it was all for a reason.*

*Maybe it was. Maybe it wasn't.*

*What I know is this:*

*something good came out of it ~*

*even if it's just that you know*

*what you're made of now.*

*That's a silver lining.*

*It's not nothing.*

*Underneath the still surface*

*everything is moving ~*

*the light, the silt,*

*the slow pull of current.*

*Stillness is not nothing.*

*Stillness is everything happening*

*quietly.*

*I've learned to trust*

*the still parts of myself.*

*They are not empty.*

*They are working.*

*The moss doesn't mind the shadow.*

*It made a home of it.*

*It grows where nothing flashy grows ~*

*quietly, patiently,*

*making the floor soft*

*for everything that walks over it.*

*I want to be that kind of presence.*

*The soft ground.*

*The quiet green.*

*The thing that makes it easier*

*for others to move.*

*It doesn't look like waiting.*

*It looks like trust ~*

*trusting that the seed knows how to be a tree,*

*that the wound knows how to close,*

*that the answer is forming*

*even when you can't hear it yet.*

*Patience is not passive.*

*It is a radical act of faith.*

*I know you're tired.*

*I know it has been longer*

*than you thought it would be,*

*and harder than you planned for,*

*and the finish line keeps moving.*

*Keep going anyway.*

*Not because it will definitely work out.*

*Because you don't know yet*

*what you're capable of.*

*Because you haven't found out*

*what's waiting on the other side of this effort.*

*Because the only way*

*to find out*

*is to keep going.*

*So keep going.*

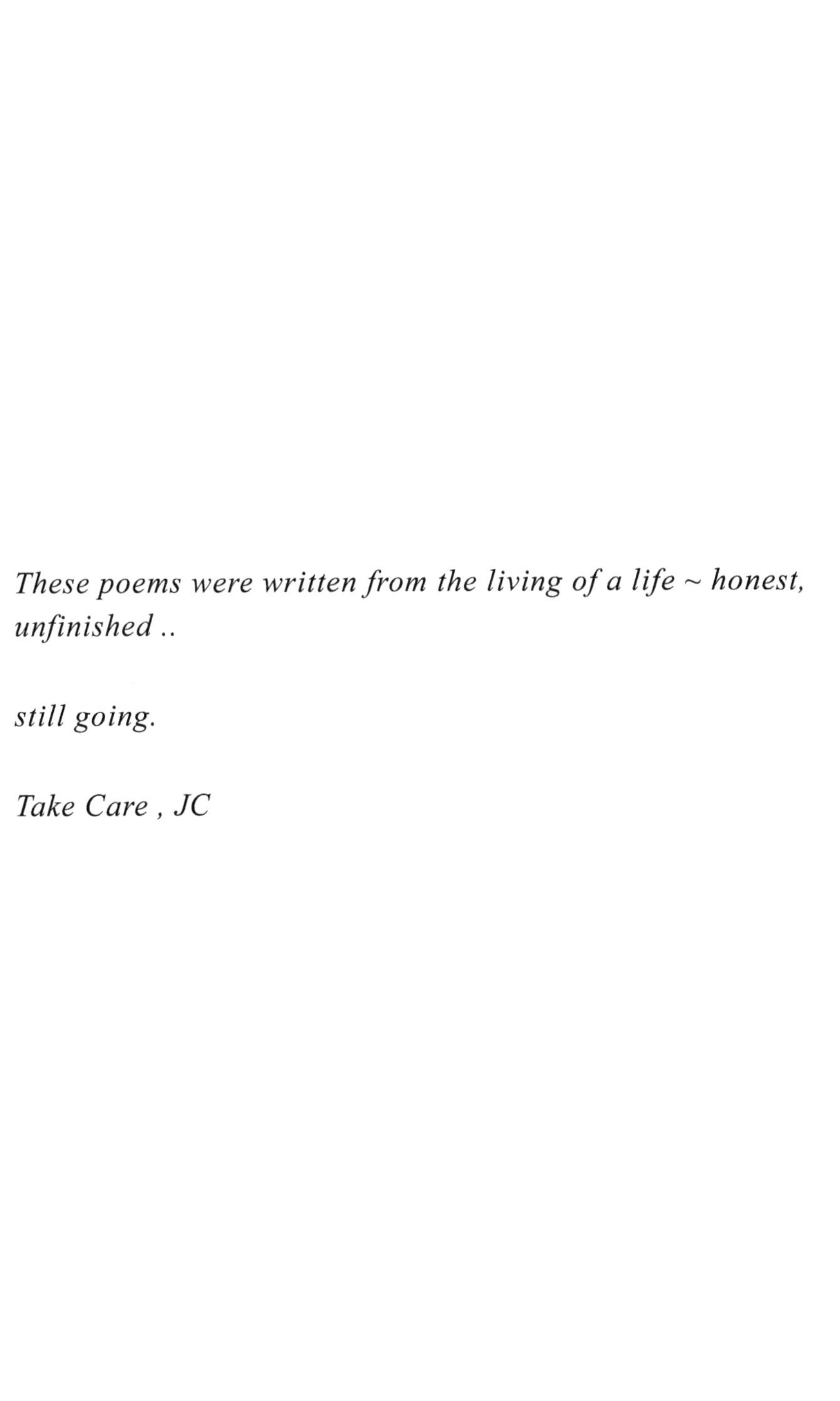

*These poems were written from the living of a life ~ honest, unfinished ..*

*still going.*

*Take Care , JC*

*& Now I Continue ..*

www.ingramcontent.com/pod-product-compliance
Ingram Content Group UK Ltd.
Pitfield, Milton Keynes, MK11 3LW, UK
UKHW041641190726
13854UKWH00006B/2635

9 798988 464884